Istanbul - 1435 / 2014

© Erkam Publications 2012 / 1433 H
ISBN: 978-9944-83-440-7

Erkam Publications
Ikitelli Organize Sanayi Bölgesi
Turgut Özal Cd. No: 117/2-C
Başakşehir, Istanbul, Turkey
Tel: (+90-212) 671-0700 pbx
Fax: (+90-212) 671-0717
E-mail: info@islamicpublishing.net
Web site: http://islamicpublishing.net

All rights reserved. No part of this publication may be reproduced, stored in a retrieval system, or transmitted in any from or by any means, electronic, mechanical, photocopying, recording or otherwise, without the prior permission of the copyright owner.

The author	: Osman Nûri Topbaş
Translator	: İsmail ERİŞ
Redactor	: Süleyman DERİN
	Joseph SHAMIS
Graphics	: Ali KAYA
Printed by	: Erkam Printhouse

101
Steps In Education

By Osman Nuri TOPBAŞ

ERKAM
PUBLICATIONS

From the Most Beautiful of Words
From THE HOLY QUR'AN:

"… do good (to others) as Allah has done good to you …"
(al-Qasas 28; 77)

"Then on that day you shall most certainly be questioned about the blessings [life, possessions, abilities, and all other means]."
(al-Takathur 102; 8)

1

Education begins in the mother's womb.
Therefore a human being's first educator
is his mother.

2

Children are divine blessings entrusted upon parents and teachers so as they equip them with goodness and high character.

3

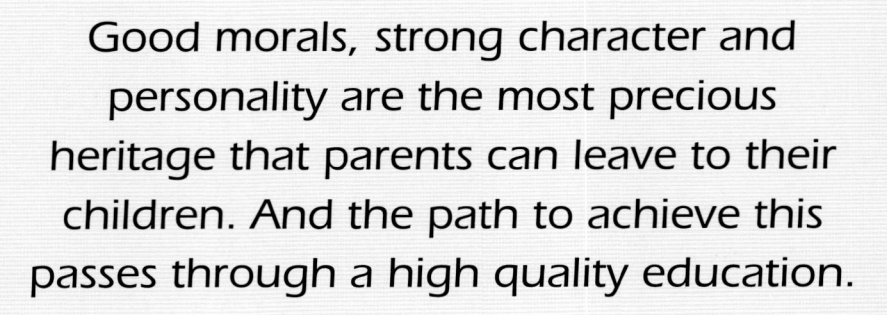

Good morals, strong character and personality are the most precious heritage that parents can leave to their children. And the path to achieve this passes through a high quality education.

4

Among creation, it is human beings who are most in need of education. The finest art in life is the raising of good human beings. Allah the Almighty sent His messengers as the greatest human educators. In other words, the task of education is a prophetic profession.

5

An educator is not just someone who gives information on a certain subject, but he is also someone who sows seeds of sincerity, opens up new horizons, invites to common sense, and teaches good manners and proper conducts. In other words, an educator is someone who builds a sound conscience in his student.

6

In order to raise a child, it is not enough to provide him with a place to sleep and food to be nourished with. What is most required is the embellishment of his mental and spiritual world with knowledge and learning.

7

An educator should educate his student with spirituality. He should arouse his student's interest, not just towards worldly sciences, but also towards religious learning, spirituality and wisdom.

8

Education given one-sidedly without spirituality is inadequate. It is necessary to keep a balance between the material and spiritual worlds. Otherwise, like a bird trying to fly with one-wing, the student will become the prey of a hungry cat.

9

For every creature that cannot keep up with the flow of life, it is inevitable to vanish in time. This is why Ali (may Allah be pleased with him) gave us the following advice:

"Raise your children not in accordance with the conditions of your time, but in accordance with the time in which they will live."

10

If a nation possesses a handful of well-trained and devoted men, it will be superior to other nations; if not, it will be backward.

11

It is not a miracle to be able to see a nation's future. To do that, it is enough to look at the children and the youth. If they spend their energy and strength in the path of goodness, spirituality, and virtues, then a bright future will be waiting for that nation. On the contrary, if they spend their energy using brute force and gratifying selfish desires, the future will be sorrowful.

12

Those who have capital look for the most efficient field to invest in. Education, however, is the most significant field to be invested in. The most correct preparation for the future is the raising of qualified and ideal human beings.

13

The first thing that a teacher should possess is a strong character that raises admiration among his students; and he should spread enlightenment, spirituality, and positive energy from his heart, and should overflow with mercy and love for his students.

14

It is impossible for a teacher to influence his students if his actions deny his words. As the famous Turkish wise man Ziya Pasha says:

"A person's works are like a mirror showing his character; so one should not be cheated by mere words."

15

An educator should first adorn his own life with the goodness that he advises to others and should try to become a living example.

16

It is necessary for an educator to spread positive energy around. In this respect even some scenes from the lives of animals are exemplary: The chicken protects its chicks under its wings while bringing them up. The snake raises its youngsters by its glances. The scorpion carries its youngsters on its back. While animals treat their offspring with such care, how should humans behave?

17

There cannot be high quality education if there is no trust between the teacher and the student. An educator, above all, should be able to present strong character to the people around him because people adorn exemplary and dignified personalities with strong character. They follow such personalities' footsteps.

18

The masses are shaped in accordance with the people leading them. The age of happiness (Asr Sa'adah) was shaped by the spiritual patterns of the Prophet (pbuh). The Companions of the Suffa are the best examples of this. Abdullah b. Mas'ud, one of the Companions of the Suffa, said showing the level of perfection he reached through the prophetic training: *"We could hear the remembrances (dhikr) of the morsels going down our throats."*

19

Spiritual gatherings to give religious advise (suhba) were the Prophet's most important method of education, for there was a deep spiritual connection in those gatherings. Such gatherings would give the spiritual nourishment that the people who joined needed. Hence giving such talks are similar to writing prescriptions for their needs.

20

An educator should consider the possibility that the student entrusted to him can be one of the prominent figures of the future; and he should not forget that some of the geniuses who can change the world are maybe under his care.

21

In order to offer high quality service, an educator should also be careful about his self-development. Effort for continuous development should be his natural characteristic. Otherwise, many gifts and talents can fade away because of his incompetence.

22

Qualified generations are the products of qualified educators who can give knowledge and good morals. Those who are trained by incompetent and unqualified teachers will turn into incompetent and weak personalities.

23

If we wish to raise perfect students, we have to be perfect educators.

24

A repaired thing is the business card of the repairman. Similarly, the quality of a teacher can be evaluated by the quality of the student whom he trained.

25

It is an important responsibility of an educator to train himself well, for a poor educator only wastes the time of the students who are entrusted to him.

26

A shepherd is responsible for his herd. He has to carry a lamb whose leg is broken. Similarly, students are the liabilities of their educators.

27

Everybody believes that their words are important and precious and they want them to be noticed. This is why an educator should carefully listen a student who comes to ask help about a problem.

28

An educator should take his student seriously, esteem him, and should let his student feel this through his actions.

29

An educator who turns his student into a little bush who had the capacity to be a big maple tree will surely be responsible before Allah.

30

An educator should know his students' characters so well that he could catch the vein that will take him to their souls.

31

Since characters and personalities are diverse, a method or a piece of advice can benefit one student, while the same method or advice could harm the other. This is why an educator should know his students' spiritual state.

32

An educator should know his students' talents and gifts like he knows the pieces of his prayer beads, to be able to guide his students towards the direction of their talents.

33

Today we are living in such times that people are unconsciously adrift like pieces of wood in flood waters. More sadly, many a river which can give life to the lands it passes through is flowing into sewers for they are not guided in the right directions.

34

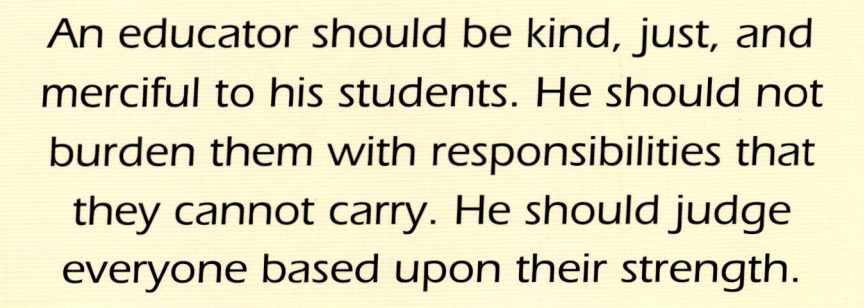

An educator should be kind, just, and merciful to his students. He should not burden them with responsibilities that they cannot carry. He should judge everyone based upon their strength.

35

A fair educator is the teacher of the entire class. There would be no peace in classes without justice; in classes without peace, no classes can be taught; in places where no classes are taught, there can be no education.

36

An educator should know well that justice does not mean treating everyone equally but giving them what they deserve. An educator should also abstain from all kinds of behavior that could harm the sense of justice.

37

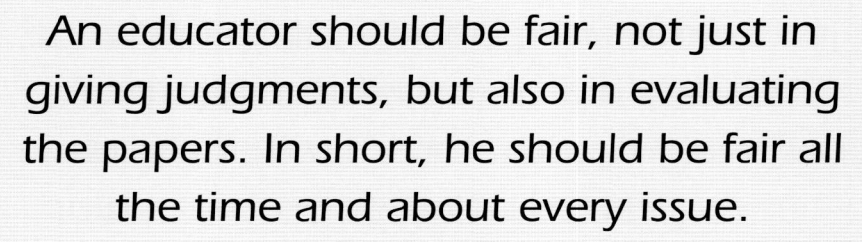

An educator should be fair, not just in giving judgments, but also in evaluating the papers. In short, he should be fair all the time and about every issue.

38

An educator should make plans according to the formation of his class and instruments of the lessons so that he can teach an efficient lesson.

39

A well planned and programmed educator can see where he stopped before, what he taught, and how much of a result he got.

40

While making plans and programs, a teacher must think about when, where, and how he will apply educational methods.

41

An educator must know his responsibility is not just the transfer of knowledge. While planning his lessons, an educator should prepare parts which will attract students' attention. Presenting lessons by giving real life examples and using the method of Q and A (question and answer) will keep students active and attentive.

42

Patience, perseverance, and self-sacrifice are the most essential keys for success in education.

43

An educator should not give up in the face of difficulties and hardships; on the contrary his endurance should be strengthened and he should get stronger under difficult conditions.

44

Because of weaknesses and lack of means, an educator should never lose hope or show carelessness and lack of energy.

45

It is necessary not to forget that the water of life is usually hidden in difficult times and places of hardships; for what makes life precious and prosperous are the efforts and sacrifices on the path of realizing a noble goal.

46

Education is not an ephemeral love. It is a lofty responsibility which should be fulfilled with love and eagerness until the last breath. In this respect patience should be the nourishment of an educator and God should be his support.

47

An educator is a person who can protect his faith in whatever community he is in; who can keep his heart away from concerns of property and benefit; who can hear the silent voices of those who scream in need for education.

48

Just like it is a mistake to neglect one's children, parents, and profession for earning his livelihood with the excuse of serving others, it is also a mistake to use such things as an excuse to run away from helping others.

49

An educator should neither be sad for missed material opportunities, nor be happy and get spoiled from having an abundance of worldly possessions.

50

An educator should spare time for his students outside the classroom hours. He should not be like a worker clocking in and out and looking forward to the end of his shift.

51

An educator should not be a problem creator but a problem solver. Instead of looking for mistakes and deficiencies by criticizing, he should be able to approach matters with a positive spirit and perspective.

52

An educator should not blame others for faults during the process of education; he should look at himself as the source of such faults.

53

To an educator, looking for excuses by saying "what can I do? I have no talents. These are spoiled times. No one is coming to my classes," God Almighty responds to such excuses by creating fig-trees out of rock-walls and producing fruits from them.

54

Education is the art of forgetting excuses before all kinds of hardships. Education cannot be achieved where intolerance and excuses come into the picture.

55

A good educator should not wait for chances and possibilities to come to him. He should always be in search of ways to serve others.

56

Education is not a profession of sitting and waiting. It requires a high level of energy. Therefore the educator must fill his heart with positive energy.

57

Seeds of knowledge sown with love and eagerness will become the great sycamore trees of the future.

58

An educator should know well the good manners accepted and respected by the community and should never neglect them.

59

An elegant, polite, and fine hearted educator should serve others with the excitement of worship; he should not hurt the feelings of others and should not let his own feelings be hurt easily. It should not be forgotten that hearts are the places of Divine sight.

60

An educator should be careful about his every action and behavior. He should be polite even when he is making jokes.

61

A good educator should know the delicate borders between candidness and levity, modesty and humiliation, dignity and pride. He should not confuse them with each other.

62

An educator should act and behave in every step of life in a way suitable to Islamic character. He should not forget that every one of his acts and every one of his words are like bricks placed into the structure of his students' personality.

63

An educator should know that education is not just the transfer of knowledge, but also a transfer of behavior. He should think about the mistakes and faults that may also be copied during this transfer process and should always feel the responsibility of transferring inappropriate acts and behaviors.

64

An educator should be a person of hearts who tries to reach Divine forgiveness through forgiving others.

65

Everyone is in need of affection and kindness. Showing kindness and love to human beings decreases the enmities of enemies and increases the love and affinity of friends.

66

An appropriate education cannot be fulfilled by rude, heartbreaking, and harsh methods.

67

It is never acceptable for an educator to tyrannize those under his commands for the sake of discipline.

68

Excessive harshness creates grudges. Excessive tolerance weakens authority. Success becomes possible by keeping a good balance between them.

69

An educator should say his words kindly and nicely and always talk about goodness. For no one likes harsh words and rudeness. Humbleness, kindness, and sweet talk are the best way to enter the hearts.

70

Just like a pilot who does not feel physiologically well cannot be allowed to fly a plane, an angry educator or someone who is morally down should not be allowed to enter the classroom.

71

An educator should make his warnings and give his advice peacefully and should not forget that acts and behaviors hurting others' feelings are the greatest personality weaknesses.

72

Human beings are always under the influence of their feelings. They think and make decisions under their influence. Therefore, a good educator should always make decisions after consulting others. This enables him to give the right services.

73

The effects of an educator whose heart is filled with love and spirituality are like the effects of a breeze blowing over gardens filled with fragrant flowers and taking their nice perfume to faraway places.

74

This world turns into Paradise by three things: by the overflowing of mercy through your hands, the tongue, and the heart ...

75

In order to reach salvation, mature believers search for others in their societies to give them education, service, and mercy so as to save them.

76

The real conquest is the conquest of hearts. And this can only be achieved by those who turn their hearts into convents of love.

77

An exemplary educator is an expert of hearts. He is a doctor inoculating the souls with the vaccine of eternal life.

78

The heart of an educator should turn into a spiritual center of rehabilitation by gaining the ability to look at creation through the sight of its Creator.

79

Love and hard work solve all problems. We win the people whose problems we solve. We gain the spiritual rewards for everyone whom we win and carry the heavy responsibility of everyone we lose.

80

Sacrifice is the measure for love. Just talking means nothing. Mawlana Jalaladdin Rumi says:
"Do not become a fool of words." Claim of love needs to be proven by sacrifices.

81

An educator should feel his students' pains and become happy with their joys. He should accept them as friends, brothers, and sisters. He should also be aware of the language of friendship and brotherhood.

82

An educator should not be someone looking for his students' mistakes and deficiencies; rather he should be someone trying to correct their mistakes by not revealing them.

83

Love is like a power line between two hearts. Soundness of education depends on the strength of this line.

84

An educator must open the gates of his heart to the students so wide that they can establish a strong line of influence.

85

Love for an educator increases the interest in what he teaches. Approaching students with love and mercy enables the educator to transfer his message, not through the channels of reason, but through the channels of heart.

86

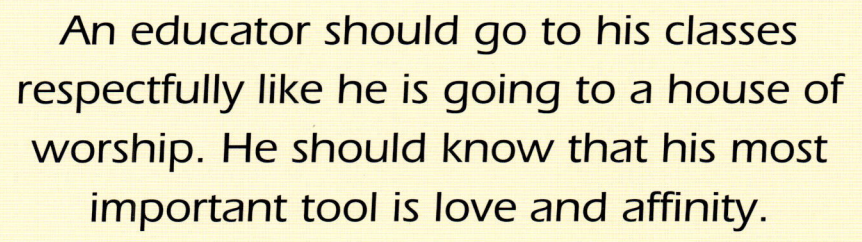

An educator should go to his classes respectfully like he is going to a house of worship. He should know that his most important tool is love and affinity.

87

Knowledge which does not reach the heart cannot turn into wisdom.

88

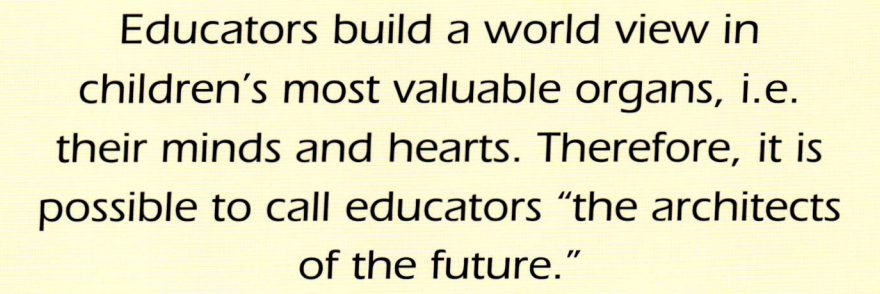

Educators build a world view in children's most valuable organs, i.e. their minds and hearts. Therefore, it is possible to call educators "the architects of the future."

89

Knowledge and wisdom can only be taught and become effective through living with a pious and deep heart. When someone achieves this state, he sees his students through the lenses of love and mercy. Seeds sown with love and mercy becomes eternal.

90

In order to be a good educator, one should have strong feelings of love and mercy.

91

Students should be seen as wounded birds and treated with kindness and mercy. For kindness and mercy are the most effective and powerful medicine for raising sound minds and hearts.

92

Mercy is like an inextinguishable fire in the educator's heart.

93

It is oppression to humanity to appoint as educators those who are self-seeking and deprived of mercy and kindness.

94

Just like scenes of roses and flowers make the harshest people and grimmest faces smile, people guiding others should have characters like roses and flowers. They should be able to soften the toughest hearts and make the grimmest faces smile.

95

The most important issue that an educator needs to pay attention to is knowing that faults are from himself and successes are from his Lord.

96

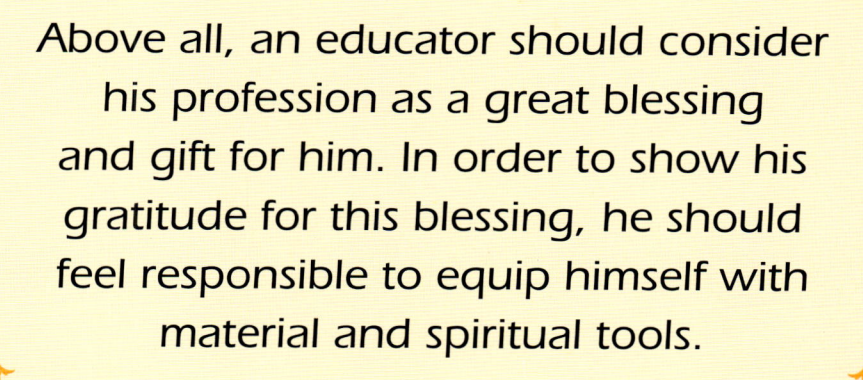

Above all, an educator should consider his profession as a great blessing and gift for him. In order to show his gratitude for this blessing, he should feel responsible to equip himself with material and spiritual tools.

97

"Selfishness" and "pretension" should leave their places to "love" and "kindness" in an educator.

98

The life of an educator should be based on sincerity, effort, and service free from pride.

99

Every day is a new and clean page from the calendar of life. It is in your hands to fill this clean page in the best way.

100

An educator should treat every moment with his students like it is his last breath in this world and thus he should spend that moment in the best way possible. He should feel grateful and show his gratitude in his actions.

101

Children are in need of their parents' and teachers' education in this world, while parents and teachers are in need of their children's prayers and continuous charity *(sadaqa jariya)* in the Hereafter.

From the best guidance of education
THE HOLY QUR'AN and THE TRADITIONS OF THE MESSENGER OF ALLAH

The best of words is the Book of Allah.

The best of paths is the path of the Messenger of Allah.

Piety is the soundest shelter.

The noblest speech is the remembrance of Allah.

The most beautiful stories are in the Holy Qur'an.

Enlightened paths are the paths of guidance of Prophets.

The best and most beneficial knowledge is the one that turns into wisdom.

Little wealth for which proper gratitude is shown is better than abundant wealth for which no gratitude is shown.

The worst excuse is the one presented at the time of death.

The worst regret is the one shown on the Day of Judgment.

Lying is the gravest sin.

The best richness is the richness of heart and to get rich through satisfaction.

The best faith is the one engraved into the hearts.

Wealth without charity and alms will be a shame on the Day of Judgment.

Usury and loan sharking are the worst types of earning.

The darkest blindness is to lose the way after entering the right path.

The worst blindness is the blindness of the heart.

To guide a non-believer to the right path (Islam) is better than everything upon which the sun rises and sets. This is the fruit of educating the heart.

Although all kinds of waste are worse than one another;, the worst one of them is to "waste human beings."